homemade *chocolate*
in the **raw** ♥

raw, vegan, superfood & herbal recipes
Lauren Amerson
Photos by Madelene Farin

Homemade Chocolate in the Raw

Published by
Lauren Amerson

www.LaurenAmerson.com

Printed and bound in the United States of America

ISBN- 13: 978-0989432504
ISBN- 10: 0989432505

First Edition

Text © Lauren Amerson
Photographs © Madelene Farin

gratitude

Thanks to my lovely friends and family who have supported and believed in me all the way. A special thanks go out to Mom, Dad, Jen, Alicia, and Jon!

Thanks to the very generous people who backed my Kickstarter.com project that funded the making of this book: Sunil Rajan, Brett Herford-Fell, Mike Williams, Crystal Sharp, Rooney, Jason Hermans, Jennifer Parrish, Terry, Sandro Turriate, Chad Ferguson, John Mellgren, Adrienne Dorias, Jason McTiernan, Kate, Steven McVeigh, Matt Larkowski, Donnie Ashworth, Jon Repole, Graham Ryan, Tracy Revels, Daniel Dalerhult, Dan Bodenstien, Chef Seth Evan Kirschbaum, Bryan Willauber, Gidget London, Ashley Reekie, Mary Sexton, Hughes Sellier, JMFM0911, Linda, Kyriacos Souroullas, Damon Anderson, Peyman Oreizy, Phil Larkowski, Chris R. Martin, Peter Easton, Henrick Koskinen, Trent Gruenwald, Chi-Kai Chien, Kristina Bjoran, Ang, Janet Stover, Karen, Mary-Alice Pomputius, and Rebecca Sweeney Krokoski.

Thanks Madelene Farin for your amazing photography!

I am grateful for the opportunity to put so much of myself into something, and share it with all of you.

"If more of us valued food and cheer and song above hoarded gold, it would be a merrier world."

— *J.R.R. Tolkien*

contents

introduction

IN THIS SECTION, YOU WILL BE
INTRODUCED TO CACAO, AND THE
COMPONENTS OF MAKING RAW
CHOCOLATE
FUN AND POWERFUL!

hello!

This book is intended to serve as a recipe resource and inspiration! Beyond my personal recipes, you'll find the building blocks for creating your very own unique and tasty cacao-blessed goodies, right in your own home. I have attempted to make raw vegan chocolate fun, healthy and accessible. Anyone can make it, enjoy it, and share it.

I have created a companion page on my website for this book: LaurenAmerson.com/chocolate

It includes:

1. A growing list of physical stores which carry raw cacao, superfood, and herbal ingredients.
2. Direct links to the websites I recommend for ingredients, tools, equipment, and molds.

My mom remarked recently, "Food tastes better when you've made a mess." I totally agree! I encourage you to experiment. Don't be afraid to make a mess! Start creating your own recipes. There are endless possibilities.

Now, go play with your food!

"Experimenting isn't about trying to get a specific outcome. It's just about seeing what happens when you try something new."
— Paul Amerson

cacao as medicine

Recently, raw cacao has been acknowledged for its many beneficial properties. It's now considered one the top superfoods! It's incredibly high in magnesium, antioxidants, and has been noted for its aphrodisiac and feel-good effects. There's no doubt that raw cacao is powerful!

Without adding sweetener and salt, pure, raw cacao is slightly bitter. Bitterness is a marker of a medicinal plant. It indicates certain medicinal and nutritional properties. It also makes it impossible to be over-consumed in this bitter state.

what makes it raw?

Cacao beans used in conventional chocolate are roasted. The process for melting it down further removes it from "raw food" standards. Buy only products labeled raw when making these recipes. Raw cacao products are never roasted. The melting process for these recipes ensures that the ingredients are never heated above the raw threshold (between $110 - 120$ °F).

are the herbs raw?

Since cacao amplifies the effects of medicinal herbs and superfoods, I've included some of these awesome ingredients in my recipes. Certain herbs go through a process of heat extraction to crack the cell walls, in order to make the nutrients and medicinal components more available to us. In the historic use of these herbs, this process proves to be non-damaging, and actually more effective than consuming them unprocessed. Ingredients that are not raw will be marked.

forms of cacao

Cacao beans can be purchased whole, with or without their skins. Cacao beans grow covered in a white fruit pulp, inside of a large pod, which hangs from the cacao tree.

Cacao nibs are crushed-up cacao beans.

Cacao paste is the result of grinding cacao beans into a liquid and letting it become solid again. Once in this form, it can be melted.

Cacao powder is the fiber from the cacao bean that is left when fat is pressed out.

Cacao butter is the fat pressed out from the cacao bean.

organic

In general, but especially with chocolate, it's important that the ingredients be organic. Organic goods are much higher quality and don't carry with them the long-lasting, devastating effects of conventionally-farmed products.

sweeteners

For consistency, I've chosen to use just one sweetener for all of my recipes: raw coconut nectar. It offers a unique flavor, and has the syrupy consistency that I love. I encourage you to experiment with other raw sweeteners. Adjust the quantity to your individual sweetness preference.

gratitude ritual

Before eating or drinking, I close my eyes and inwardly say a few words of gratitude for what I am about to consume.

The purpose of this ritual is simply to cultivate gratitude, and to infuse the food or drink with love, appreciation, and intention. This immediately changes your vibration, and the vibration of what you are about to consume. It also serves as a personal intention and affirmation: that you choose to eat and drink things that are good for your body, full of energy, and nutrients.

Try it out and create your own version!

"Let food be thy medicine and medicine be thy food."
— Hippocrates

foundations

THE FOLLOWING RECIPES AND
TECHNIQUES ARE FOUNDATIONAL FOR
MANY OF THE RECIPES IN THIS BOOK.
THEY ALSO HAVE OTHER USES IN RAW
VEGAN CUISINE.

melting your chocolate

Here are two methods I recommend for melting chocolate so that it remains raw.

double boiler method

You can purchase sets that are specifically made for double boiling, or you can create a setup with what you have.

1. Place a small pot on the stovetop and fill it partially with water.
2. Place a glass or metal mixing bowl on top. The bowl should be wider than the pot, and should sit over the pot, so that it does not come into direct contact with the water. The hot water in the pot will warm the bowl.
3. Put the chocolate into the top bowl.On high heat, bring the water to a simmer.
4. Then, reduce to low-medium heat, keeping it at a simmer.
5. As the chocolate begins to melt, whisk slowly and continuously. Whisking speeds up melting, and avoids overheating.
6. Once chocolate is melted, turn off the heat and remove the bowl from the stove, using a towel or oven mitt.

dehydrator method

This method is for a tray-style food dehydrator (see the tips & resources chapter).

1. Put the chocolate into a mixing bowl.
2. Remove enough trays from the dehydrator to fit your bowl. Place the uncovered bowl inside.
3. Turn the dehydrator to 115 °F, and close it.
4. Whisk occasionally, until the chocolate is melted.
5. Turn off the heat and remove the bowl from dehydrator.

tempering

Tempering is a technique used to create tight organization of the fat crystals in chocolate. It gives chocolate a snap, makes it shiny and smooth, and allows it to remain solid at room temperature.

Tempering raw chocolate can be a tricky skill to master. It's not required for the recipes in this book. But, if you want to take your chocolate-making up a notch, here's a technique that's simple enough to do in any home kitchen. You'll need a candy thermometer.

1. In a mixing bowl, melt cacao paste and cacao butter together, two-thirds of the way (use dehydrator or double boiler method).
2. Remove from heat and continue to whisk until completely melted.
3. Whisk in remaining recipe ingredients.
4. Keep whisking until the temperature drops to 80 °F.
5. Return to dehydrator or double boiler briefly, to bring mixture up to 88 – 90 °F.
6. Remove from heat.
7. Use chocolate immediately.

preparing nuts & seeds

If you want to enjoy raw nuts or seeds, make raw nut/seed butters, or make raw nut/seed mylk, it's important to know how to prepare them. Almost all raw nuts and seeds have a coating of enzyme inhibitors and phytic acid. This serves to prevent germination until the conditions are ideal in nature (mainly, that there's sufficient water around). We mimic this moist state with the soaking process. Soaking nuts or seeds in water for a sufficient period of time removes the coating. This starts the germination process, which brings the dormant nut or seed to life, and makes them more bioavailable to humans. Each type of nut or seed requires a different soaking period.

soaking

1. Place nuts or seeds in a bowl.
2. Cover them in water for the recommended length of time.
3. Pour them into a strainer and rinse.
4. Use them immediately, or store them in a closed container in the fridge.

Soaking changes the texture of nuts and seeds, as they absorb water and soften. For a crunchy nut or seed, do the full preparation as follows. You will need a dehydrator.

full preparation

1. Soak, rinse, and strain the nuts/seeds (as described above).
2. Spread them evenly over dehydrator trays, only one layer thick.
3. Dehydrate them at 115 °F for 24 hours.
4. Use them immediately, or store them in closed container in dry place.

making nut & seed mylk

ingredients

- 2½ cups soaked nuts/seeds
- 6 dates, pitted
- 5½ cups water

directions

1. Blend all ingredients in a high-speed blender for about one minute.
2. Strain it through a nut milk bag into a large bowl.
3. Use immediately, or store in sealed container in the fridge, or freeze in ice cube trays.

notes

This recipe makes about 7 cups and will last about five days in the fridge.

This recipe can be made in smaller batches.

If you have nut or seed mylk that will go bad before you can use it all, just freeze it in ice cube trays. Then you can use it anytime in mylk shakes, smoothies, and ice creams.

The dates in this recipe make it a sweetened nut or seed mylk, which is what all the recipes in this book call for. For unsweetened, simply leave out the dates.

The pulp that is left over can be made into a flour. Spread the wet pulp on dehydrator trays with ParaFlexx sheets and dehydrate on 115 °F for 8 hours. Then, blend into a fine flour in Vitamix blender, using tamper.

making nut & seed butter

ingredients

- 4 – 6 cups fully prepared nuts or seeds (page 18)

directions

1. Do a full preparation of your choice of nuts or seeds.
2. Put the nuts or seeds in the Vitamix blender. The blender must be completely dry.
3. Start the blender on low. Use the tamper to press contents down into blades as you turn it up to high. Use the tamper continuously while the blender is on.
4. When the blender gets warm, stop. Open the lid and let it cool for at least 30 minutes.
5. Repeat Steps 3 and 4 until the contents have reached a smooth, silky texture. For harder nuts like almonds, it may take up to eight repetitions.
6. Use immediately, or store in sealed container in fridge.

notes

Making your own raw nut or seed butters can take several hours in the Vitamix.

You can apply the same method using a food processor. In my experience, the food processor doesn't yield results that are as smooth as the Vitamix. High-quality stone grinders yield the best results, but are very expensive, break easily, and have limited uses.

"If you really want to make a friend, go to someone's house and eat with him... the people who give you their food give you their heart."
— *Cesar Chavez*

molded chocolates & bark

THE RECIPES IN THIS SECTION UTILIZE MOLDS, WHICH COME IN A VARIETY OF SHAPES AND SIZES. REFER TO MY WEBSITE FOR A LIST OF THE ONES I'VE USED HERE.

basic molded chocolate

ingredients

- ½ cup raw cacao paste, finely chopped
- ¼ cup raw cacao butter, finely chopped
- 1½ tbsp raw coconut nectar
- ¼ tsp vanilla powder
- dash of salt

directions

1. Melt the cacao butter and cacao paste (use double boiler or dehydrator method).
2. Whisk in the remaining ingredients until smooth.
3. Pour the chocolate into a mold, supported underneath with a cutting board or tray.
4. Put it in the freezer for at least 30 minutes to harden.
5. Pop the chocolates out and Enjoy immediately, or store them in the fridge.

"All you need is love. But a little chocolate now and then doesn't hurt."

— Charles M. Schulz

chlorella turmeric

ingredients

- $\frac{1}{2}$ cup cacao paste, finely chopped
- $\frac{1}{4}$ cup cacao butter, finely chopped
- $1\frac{1}{2}$ tbsp raw coconut nectar
- $1\frac{1}{2}$ tsp chlorella powder
- $\frac{1}{2}$ tsp turmeric powder
- 1 tsp vanilla powder
- dash of salt

directions

1. Melt the cacao butter and cacao paste (use double boiler or dehydrator method).
2. Whisk in the remaining ingredients until smooth.
3. Pour the chocolate into a mold, supported underneath with a cutting board or tray.
4. Put it in the freezer for at least 30 minutes to harden.
5. Pop the chocolates out and Enjoy immediately, or store them in the fridge.

cordyceps maca bark

ingredients

- ½ cup raw cacao paste, finely chopped
- ¼ cup raw cacao butter, finely chopped
- 1½ tbsp raw coconut nectar
- ½ tbsp Maca Bliss* (by Longevity Power) or raw maca powder
- ½ tbsp cordyceps powder or extract
- ½ tsp vanilla powder
- dash of salt
- 1 tbsp raw cacao nibs
- 2 tbsp raw macadamia nuts (or other nuts), chopped

directions

1. Prepare the mold: line a square or rectangular container with plastic wrap. (The wider the container, the thinner the bark. I prefer a 3" × 3" or 4" × 4" container.)
2. Sprinkle one-third of the macadamia nuts into the bottom of the mold.
3. Melt the cacao butter and cacao paste (use double boiler or dehydrator method).
4. Whisk in the remaining ingredients until smooth, excluding the nibs and macadamia nuts.
5. Whisk in cacao nibs.
6. Pour the chocolate into the mold.
7. Sprinkle the remaining macadamia nuts on top.
8. Put it in the freezer for at least 30 minutes to harden.
9. Chop the bark into pieces, or break with your hands.
10. Enjoy immediately, or store in the fridge.

notes

* This ingredient is not raw.

cayenne carob

ingredients

- ½ cup raw cacao paste, finely chopped
- ¼ cup raw cacao butter, finely chopped
- 1½ tbsp raw coconut nectar
- ½ tbsp raw carob powder
- ½ tsp Maca Bliss* (by Longevity Power) or raw maca powder
- ½ tsp ground cinnamon
- ¼ tsp vanilla powder
- ⅛ tsp cayenne powder
- dash of salt

directions

1. Melt the cacao butter and cacao paste (use double boiler or dehydrator method).
2. Whisk in the remaining ingredients until smooth.
3. Pour the chocolate into a mold, supported underneath with a cutting board or tray.
4. Put it in the freezer for at least 30 minutes to harden.
5. Pop the chocolates out and Enjoy immediately, or store them in the fridge.

notes

* This ingredient is not raw.

pecan sesame crunch bar

ingredients

- ½ cup raw cacao paste, finely chopped
- ¼ cup raw cacao butter, finely chopped
- 1½ tbsp raw coconut nectar
- 1 tsp raw mesquite powder
- dash of salt
- 2 tbsp fully prepared raw pecans, chopped
- 1 tsp raw sesame seeds
- 1 tsp raw cacao nibs

directions

1. Melt the cacao butter and cacao paste (use double boiler or dehydrator method).
2. Whisk in coconut nectar, mesquite powder, and salt until smooth.
3. Whisk in remaining ingredients.
4. Pour the chocolate into a mold, supported underneath with a cutting board or tray.
5. Put it in the freezer for at least 30 minutes to harden.
6. Pop the chocolates out and Enjoy immediately, or store them in the fridge.

longevity coconut bar

ingredients

chocolate:
- ½ cup raw cacao paste, finely chopped
- ¼ cup raw cacao butter, finely chopped
- 1½ tbsp raw coconut nectar
- ½ tsp vanilla powder
- 1 tsp Longevity in a Bottle* (by Longevity Power)
- ¼ tsp turmeric powder
- ½ tsp raw lucuma powder
- dash of salt

topping:
- raw shredded coconut

directions

1. Melt the cacao butter and cacao paste (use double boiler or dehydrator method).
2. Whisk in the remaining ingredients until smooth.
3. Pour the chocolate into a mold, supported underneath with a cutting board or tray.
4. Top generously with shredded coconut.
5. Put it in the freezer for at least 30 minutes to harden.
6. Gently brush off the excess coconut.
7. Pop the chocolates out and Enjoy immediately, or store them in the fridge.

notes

* This ingredient is not raw.

peppermint cream

ingredients

coating:
- ½ batch "basic molded chocolate" (page 26)

peppermint cream:
- ½ cup raw coconut butter, finely chopped
- ½ cup raw cacao butter, finely chopped
- 2 tsp raw coconut nectar
- 14 drops peppermint essential oil (organic, therapeutic grade)
- dash of salt

directions

1. Prepare peppermint cream: melt the cacao butter and coconut butter (use double boiler or dehydrator method).
2. Whisk in the remaining ingredients until smooth.
3. Pour the cream ¼-inch thick, into a circular mold, supported underneath with cutting board or tray.
4. Put it in the freezer for at least 30 minutes to harden.
5. Prepare the "basic molded chocolate" recipe through Step 2.
6. Pour the chocolate into a small bowl.
7. Carefully pop the hardened cream out of the mold.
8. Put parchment paper on the cutting board or tray.
9. Submerge the hardened cream in chocolate and lift out with fork, letting the excess chocolate drip into the bowl.
10. Place on parchment paper. Once all are coated, put cutting board or tray in freezer to harden chocolate for at least 30 minutes.
11. Enjoy immediately, or store in the fridge.

notes

Try adding spirulina or cacao nibs to peppermint cream.

nut butter cups

ingredients

chocolate:
- 1 batch "basic molded chocolate" recipe (page 26)

filling:
- 3 tbsp raw almond butter
- 1½ tsp raw coconut nectar
- dash of salt

directions

1. Place your mold in the freezer while you prepare the chocolate.
2. Prepare the "basic molded chocolate" recipe through Step 2.
3. Remove the mold from the freezer. Place it on a cutting board or tray for support.
4. Use only half of the total chocolate for this step! Fill one mold cavity one-third full with chocolate. Using your finger, gently coat the inner sides of the mold with the chocolate you've poured in. The chocolate will begin to harden. Repeat, one at a time, for each mold cavity.
5. Put it in the freezer for at least 10 minutes to harden.
6. Mix the filling ingredients and roll it into ½ tsp size balls.
7. Remove the mold from freezer and drop one filling ball into the center of each cavity.
8. Pour in the remaining chocolate to fill the mold.
9. Put it in the freezer for at least 30 minutes to harden.
10. Pop the chocolates out. Enjoy immediately, or store them in the fridge.

notes

Try adding superfood powder, herbs, or spices to the filling.

lime-filled

ingredients

chocolate:
- 1 batch "basic molded chocolate" recipe (page 26)

filling:
- 2 tbsp raw almond butter
- ½ tbsp raw coconut nectar
- 2½ tsp fresh lime juice
- 1 tsp lime zest (must be organic)
- dash of salt

directions

1. Place your mold in the freezer while you prepare the chocolate.
2. Prepare the "basic molded chocolate" recipe through Step 2.
3. Remove the mold from the freezer. Place it on a cutting board or tray for support.
4. Use only half of the total chocolate for this step! Fill one mold cavity one-third full with chocolate. Using your finger, gently coat the inner sides of the mold with the chocolate you've poured in. The chocolate will begin to harden. Repeat, one at a time, for each mold cavity.
5. Put it in the freezer for at least 10 minutes to harden.
6. Mix the filling ingredients and scoop into a small piping bag (page 134).
7. Remove the mold from the freezer and squeeze about ½ tsp into each cavity. With a little lime juice on your finger, press down on the filling lightly so that it is below the level of the top of the mold.
8. Pour in the remaining chocolate to fill in mold.
9. Put it in the freezer for at least 30 minutes to harden.
10. Pop the chocolates out. Enjoy immediately, or store them in the fridge.

chocolate
layer bars

FOR THE RECIPES IN THIS SECTION, I
PREFER TO USE A SQUARE MOLD OR
FLOWER MOLD. THE RECIPES ARE
WRITTEN FOR A THREE-LAYER BAR. TO
CONVERT TO A TWO LAYER RECIPE,
EITHER DIVIDE THE CHOCOLATE IN
HALF OR DOUBLE THE FLAVORED
LAYER.

coconut lemon

ingredients

chocolate layer:
- 1 batch "basic molded chocolate" recipe (page 26)

coconut lemon layer:
- ¼ cup raw coconut butter
- 2 tbsp raw coconut oil
- 2 tsp raw coconut nectar
- 2 tsp lemon zest (must be organic)
- dash of salt

directions

1. Prepare the "basic molded chocolate" recipe through Step 2.
2. Using half of the total chocolate, fill the mold cavities one-third full, supported with a cutting board or tray underneath.
3. Put it in the freezer for at least 20 minutes to harden.
4. In the meantime, prepare the coconut lemon layer: in a small bowl, melt the coconut butter and coconut oil using double boiler or dehydrator.
5. Add the remaining ingredients and whisk until smooth. This mixture should be thick, but pourable.
6. Remove the mold from the freezer and fill another one-third full with the coconut lemon mixture.
7. Return it to the freezer for at least 10 minutes to harden.
8. Remove the mold from the freezer and fill the last one-third full with remaining chocolate.
9. Return it to the freezer for at least 20 minutes to harden.
10. Pop the chocolates out. Enjoy immediately, or store them in the fridge.

notes

Recipe is shown on page 48.

blue-green algae

ingredients

chocolate layer:
- 1 batch "basic molded chocolate" recipe (page 26)

blue-green layer:
- 3 tbsp raw cashew butter
- 2 tbsp raw cacao butter
- 1 tbsp raw coconut nectar
- 1 tsp blue-green algae
- ½ tsp vanilla powder
- 1 tbsp raw lucuma powder
- dash of salt

directions

1. Prepare the "basic molded chocolate" recipe through Step 2.
2. Using half of the total chocolate, fill the mold cavities one-third full, supported with a cutting board or tray underneath.
3. Put it in the freezer for at least 20 minutes to harden.
4. In the meantime, prepare the blue-green layer: in a small bowl, melt the cashew butter and cacao butter (use double boiler or dehydrator method).
5. Add the remaining ingredients and whisk until smooth. This mixture should be thick, but pourable.
6. Remove the mold from the freezer and fill another one-third full with the blue-green mixture.
7. Return it to the freezer for at least 10 minutes to harden.
8. Remove the mold from the freezer and fill the last one-third full with remaining chocolate.
9. Return it to the freezer for at least 20 minutes to harden.
10. Pop the chocolates out. Enjoy immediately, or store them in the fridge.

notes

Recipe is shown on page 48.

coconut lemon, blue-green algae, goji, matcha
layer bars

goji

ingredients

chocolate layer:
- 1 batch "basic molded chocolate" recipe (page 26)

goji layer:
- 3 tbsp raw cashew butter
- 2 tbsp raw cacao butter
- 1 tbsp raw coconut nectar
- 2 tbsp raw goji powder
- dash of salt
- ½ tbsp dried goji berries (optional)

directions

1. Prepare the "basic molded chocolate" recipe through Step 2.
2. Using half of the total chocolate, fill the mold cavities one-third full, supported with a cutting board or tray underneath.
3. Put it in the freezer for at least 20 minutes to harden.
4. In the meantime, prepare the goji layer: in a small bowl, melt the cashew butter and cacao butter (use double boiler or dehydrator method).
5. Add the remaining ingredients and whisk until smooth. This mixture should be thick, but pourable.
6. Optional: Whisk in the dried goji berries.
7. Remove the mold from the freezer and fill another one-third full with the goji mixture.
8. Return it to the freezer for at least 10 minutes to harden.
9. Remove the mold from the freezer and fill the last one-third full with remaining chocolate.
10. Return it to the freezer for at least 20 minutes to harden.
11. Pop the chocolates out. Enjoy immediately, or store them in the fridge.

matcha

ingredients

chocolate layer:
- 1 batch "basic molded chocolate" recipe (page 26)

matcha layer:
- 3 tbsp raw cashew butter
- 2 tbsp raw cacao butter
- 1 tbsp raw coconut nectar
- 2 tsp matcha powder
- dash of salt

directions

1. Prepare the "basic molded chocolate" recipe through Step 2.
2. Using half of the total chocolate, fill the mold cavities one-third full, supported with a cutting board or tray underneath.
3. Put it in the freezer for at least 20 minutes to harden.
4. In the meantime, prepare the matcha layer: in a small bowl, melt the cashew butter and cacao butter (use double boiler or dehydrator method).
5. Add the remaining ingredients and whisk until smooth. This mixture should be thick, but pourable.
6. Remove the mold from the freezer and fill another one-third full with the matcha mixture.
7. Return it to the freezer for at least 10 minutes to harden.
8. Remove the mold from the freezer and fill the last one-third full with remaining chocolate.
9. Return it to the freezer for at least 20 minutes to harden.
10. Pop the chocolates out. Enjoy immediately, or store them in the fridge.

notes

Recipe is shown on page 48.

lavender

ingredients

chocolate layer:
- 1 batch "basic molded chocolate" recipe (page 26)

lavender layer:
- 3 tbsp raw cashew butter
- 2 tbsp raw cacao butter
- 1 tbsp raw coconut nectar
- 1 tsp lavender flowers
- 2 tsp raw lucuma powder
- 2 drops lavender essential oil (organic, therapeutic)
- dash of salt

directions

1. Prepare the "basic molded chocolate" recipe through Step 2.
2. Using half of the total chocolate, fill the mold cavities one-third full, supported with a cutting board or tray underneath.
3. Put it in the freezer for at least 20 minutes to harden.
4. In the meantime, prepare the lavender layer: in a small bowl, melt the cashew butter and cacao butter (use double boiler or dehydrator method).
5. Add the remaining ingredients and whisk until smooth. This mixture should be thick, but pourable.
6. Remove the mold from the freezer and fill another one-third full with the lavender mixture.
7. Return it to the freezer for at least 10 minutes to harden.
8. Remove the mold from the freezer and fill the last one-third full with remaining chocolate.
9. Return it to the freezer for at least 20 minutes to harden.
10. Pop the chocolates out. Enjoy immediately, or store them in the fridge.

notes

Recipe is shown on page 52.

cinnamon, lavender, beet vanilla layer bars

beet vanilla

ingredients

chocolate layer:
- 1 batch "basic molded chocolate" recipe (page 26)

beet layer:
- 3 tbsp raw cashew butter
- 2 tbsp raw cacao butter
- 1 tbsp raw coconut nectar
- 1 tbsp beet powder
- 1 tsp vanilla powder
- 2 tsp raw lucuma powder
- dash of salt

directions

1. Prepare the "basic molded chocolate" recipe through Step 2.
2. Using half of the total chocolate, fill the mold cavities one-third full, supported with a cutting board or tray underneath.
3. Put it in the freezer for at least 20 minutes to harden.
4. In the meantime, prepare the beet vanilla layer: in a small bowl, melt the cashew butter and cacao butter (use double boiler or dehydrator method).
5. Add the remaining ingredients and whisk until smooth. This mixture should be thick, but pourable.
6. Remove the mold from the freezer and fill another one-third full with the beet vanilla mixture.
7. Return it to the freezer for at least 10 minutes to harden.
8. Remove the mold from the freezer and fill the last one-third full with remaining chocolate.
9. Return it to the freezer for at least 20 minutes to harden.
10. Pop the chocolates out of the mold and Enjoy immediately, or store in the fridge.

cinnamon

ingredients

chocolate layer:
- 1 batch "basic molded chocolate" recipe (page 26)

cinnamon layer:
- 3 tbsp raw almond butter
- 2 tbsp raw cacao butter
- 1 tbsp raw coconut nectar
- 1 tsp ground cinnamon
- 2 tsp raw lucuma powder
- dash of salt

directions

1. Prepare the "basic molded chocolate" recipe through Step 2.
2. Using half of the total chocolate, fill the mold cavities one-third full, supported with a cutting board or tray underneath.
3. Put it in the freezer for at least 20 minutes to harden.
4. In the meantime, prepare the cinnamon layer: in a small bowl, melt the cashew butter and cacao butter (use double boiler or dehydrator method).
5. Add the remaining ingredients and whisk until smooth. This mixture should be thick, but pourable.
6. Remove the mold from the freezer and fill another one-third full with the cinnamon mixture.
7. Return it to the freezer for at least 10 minutes to harden.
8. Remove the mold from the freezer and fill the last one-third full with remaining chocolate.
9. Return it to the freezer for at least 20 minutes to harden.
10. Pop the chocolates out of the mold and Enjoy immediately, or store in the fridge.

notes

Recipe is shown on page 52.

"The only real stumbling block is fear of failure.
In cooking, you've got to have a what-the-hell attitude."

— Julia Child

chocolate
fudges

SUPER-SMOOTH NUT BUTTER IS THE
SECRET INGREDIENT FOR THE RECIPES
IN THIS SECTION. THE RESULT IS
CHOCOLATE WITH THE TEXTURE,
APPEARANCE, AND MOUTH-FEEL OF
FUDGE. YOU WILL NEED A MINI LOAF
PAN FOR THESE RECIPES.

basic fudge

ingredients

- ⅔ cup raw cacao paste, finely chopped
- ½ cup raw cacao butter, finely chopped
- ¼ cup raw almond butter
- 3 tbsp raw coconut nectar
- 1 tsp vanilla
- ½ tsp salt

directions

1. Line a mini loaf pan (5.75" × 3") with plastic wrap.
2. Melt the cacao butter and cacao paste (use double boiler or dehydrator method).
3. Whisk in the remaining ingredients until smooth. The mixture should be slightly thick.
4. Pour the chocolate into the lined loaf pan.
5. Place it in the freezer for at least one hour to harden.
6. Remove the fudge from the mold, and chill in the fridge for another hour.
7. Enjoy immediately, or store in the fridge.

"Anything is good, if it's made of chocolate."

— Jo Brand

butterscotch white chocolate fudge, basic chocolate fudge, superfood lover's chocolate fudge

butterscotch white chocolate

ingredients

- 1 cup raw cacao butter, finely chopped
- ¼ cup raw cashew butter
- 2 tbsp raw coconut nectar
- ½ cup raw lucuma powder
- ½ tsp vanilla
- ¼ tsp salt

directions

1. Line a mini loaf pan (5.75" × 3") with plastic wrap.
2. Melt the cacao butter and cashew butter (use double boiler or dehydrator method).
3. Whisk in the remaining ingredients until smooth. The mixture should be slightly thick.
4. Pour the chocolate into the lined loaf pan.
5. Place it in the freezer for at least one hour to harden.
6. Remove the fudge from the mold, and chill in the fridge for another hour.
7. Enjoy immediately, or store in the fridge.

notes

Recipe is shown on page 59.

superfood lover's

ingredients

- ⅔ cup raw cacao paste, finely chopped
- ½ cup raw cacao butter, finely chopped
- 3 tbsp raw coconut nectar
- ¼ cup raw almond butter
- 1 tsp vanilla powder
- 1 tsp turmeric powder
- 2 tsp ground cinnamon
- ½ tsp salt
- ¼ cup fully prepared raw pecans, chopped

directions

1. Line a mini loaf pan (5.75" × 3") with plastic wrap.
2. Melt the cacao butter and cacao paste (use double boiler or dehydrator method).
3. Whisk in the remaining ingredients, except pecans, until smooth. The mixture should be slightly thick.
4. Whisk in the pecans.
5. Pour the chocolate into the lined loaf pan.
6. Place it in the freezer for at least one hour to harden.
7. Remove the fudge from the mold, and chill in the fridge for another hour.
8. Enjoy immediately, or store in the fridge.

notes

Recipe is shown on page 59.

marbled raspberry

ingredients

chocolate fudge:
- ½ batch "basic chocolate fudge" recipe (page 58)

raspberry fudge:
- ¼ cup raw coconut butter, finely chopped
- ⅓ cup raw cacao butter, finely chopped
- 1½ tbsp raw coconut nectar
- ¼ tsp salt
- 2 tbsp raw cashew butter
- ½ tsp raw lucuma powder
- ½ cup fresh raspberries (or blackberries)

directions

1. Line a mini loaf pan (5.75" × 3") with plastic wrap.
2. Prepare the half "basic chocolate fudge" recipe through Step 3.
3. Make raspberry purée: blend raspberries in a blender, then pour through a strainer to remove seeds. Use 1 tbsp of the purée for the raspberry fudge mixture.
4. In a separate bowl, prepare the raspberry fudge: melt the cacao butter and coconut butter (use double boiler or dehydrator method).
5. Whisk in the remaining ingredients until smooth.
6. In the lined loaf pan, alternate pouring the two mixtures in a zigzag pattern.
7. Move a chopstick, or knife, through the mixture in a swirling or zigzag pattern to create marbling.
8. Add droplets of extra raspberry purée on top.
9. Place it in the freezer for at least one hour to harden.
10. Remove the fudge from the mold, and chill in the fridge for another hour.
11. Enjoy immediately, or store in the fridge.

earth

ingredients

- ⅔ cup raw cacao paste, finely chopped
- ½ cup raw cacao butter, finely chopped
- 3 tbsp raw coconut nectar
- ¼ cup raw almond butter
- 2 tsp zeolite clay (by Health Force)
- 2 tsp shilajit powder
- 2 tsp raw mesquite powder
- 2 tsp Maca Bliss* (by Longevity Power)
- 1 tsp vanilla powder
- 1 tsp beet root powder
- ½ tsp salt

directions

1. Line a mini loaf pan (5.75" × 3") with plastic wrap.
2. Melt the cacao butter and cacao paste (use double boiler or dehydrator method).
3. Whisk in the remaining ingredients until smooth. The mixture should be slightly thick.
4. Pour the chocolate into the lined loaf pan.
5. Place it in the freezer for at least one hour to harden.
6. Remove the fudge from the mold, and chill in the fridge for another hour.
7. Enjoy immediately, or store in the fridge.

notes

* This ingredient is not raw.

This recipe is more dense than the other fudges. For more creaminess, add more cacao butter and almond butter.

marbled blood orange

ingredients

blood orange chocolate fudge:
- ½ batch "basic chocolate fudge" recipe (page 58)
- 1 tsp blood orange zest (must be organic)

white fudge:
- ⅓ cup raw cacao butter, finely chopped
- ¼ cup raw coconut butter, chopped
- 1½ tbsp raw coconut nectar
- 2 tbsp raw cashew butter
- ¼ tsp salt
- ½ tsp blood orange juice

directions

1. Line a mini loaf pan (5.75" × 3") with plastic wrap.
2. Prepare the half "basic chocolate fudge" recipe through Step 3.
3. Whisk in orange zest.
4. In a separate bowl, prepare the white fudge: melt the cacao butter and coconut butter (use double boiler or dehydrator method).
5. Whisk in the remaining ingredients, except blood orange juice, until smooth.
6. In lined loaf pan, alternate pouring the two mixtures in a zigzag pattern.
7. Add drops of blood orange juice on top.
8. Move a chopstick, or knife, through the mixture in a swirling or zigzag pattern to create marbling.
9. Place it in the freezer for at least one hour to harden.
10. Remove the fudge from the mold, and chill in the fridge for another hour.
11. Enjoy immediately, or store in the fridge.

chocolate ice creams, smoothies & shakes

YOU WILL NEED A HIGH-SPEED BLENDER FOR THESE RECIPES. I RECOMMEND THE VITAMIX, WITH A TAMPER. SEE PAGE 135 IF YOU ARE USING AN ICE CREAM MAKER.

basic chocolate ice cream, matt's chocolate shell

basic chocolate ice cream

ingredients

- 10 cubes frozen almond or hazelnut mylk (page 20)*
- 3 tbsp raw cacao powder
- 1 tbsp raw lucuma powder
- 1 tbsp raw coconut nectar
- ½ tsp vanilla powder
- 1 tbsp fresh aloe vera gel (optional)
- dash of salt

directions

1. Prepare the almond or hazelnut mylk, and freeze it in ice cube trays until solid.
2. Place all of the ingredients in the Vitamix blender.
3. Start the blender on low. Use the tamper to press contents down into blades as you turn it up to high. Continue, until it reaches the consistency of ice cream. Do not over-blend.
4. Enjoy immediately!

notes

* The nut mylk recipe on page 20 is for a large batch, about 7 cups. You will only need about 1¼ cups of nut mylk to make 10 frozen cubes.

Top with "matt's chocolate shell" (page 111), chopped nuts, cacao nibs, shredded coconut or "buckwheat granola" (page 105).

ingredients

- 10 cubes frozen almond or hazelnut mylk (page 20)*
- ¼ tsp vanilla powder
- ¼ tsp turmeric powder
- ¼ tsp chlorella powder
- ¼ cup fresh mint leaves
- 1 tbsp fresh aloe vera (optional)
- dash of salt
- 1 – 2 tbsp raw cacao nibs or "ian & jonah's chocolate chips" (page 114)

directions

1. Prepare the almond or hazelnut mylk, and freeze it in ice cube trays until solid.
2. Place all of the ingredients in the Vitamix blender.
3. Start the blender on low. Use the tamper to press contents down into blades as you turn it up to high. Continue, until it reaches the consistency of ice cream. Do not over-blend.
4. Add the cacao nibs or chocolate chips and blend for a few seconds.
5. Enjoy immediately!

notes

*The nut mylk recipe on page 20 is for a large batch, about 7 cups. You will only need about 1¼ cups of nut mylk to make 10 frozen cubes.

Garnish with cacao nibs and fresh mint leaves.

spice up your life smoothie

ingredients

- 3 cups water
- ½ cup raw cashews, soaked 4 – 8 hours
- 3 dates
- 2 tbsp Maca Bliss* (by Longevity Power) or raw maca powder
- 2 tbsp raw cacao powder
- 2 tbsp raw cacao nibs
- 2 tbsp raw mesquite powder
- 2 tsp raw camu camu powder
- ½ tsp cayenne powder
- 1 tbsp ground cinnamon
- 1 tbsp fresh aloe vera
- dash of salt

directions

1. Blend all of the ingredients in a high-speed blender until smooth.
2. Enjoy immediately, or store in the fridge up to three days.

notes

Blend in ice cubes for a cold drink.

You can substitute cashews and water with 4 cups of nut mylk.

* This ingredient is not raw.

jon's longevity shake

ingredients

- 1 cup raw hazelnut mylk (page 20)*
- 6 cubes frozen hazelnut mylk (page 20)*
- 2 tsp raw cacao powder
- 1 tsp Maca Bliss† (by Longevity Power) or raw maca powder
- 1 tsp vanilla powder
- 1 date
- 1 tsp raw lucuma powder
- 1 tsp Longevity in a Bottle† (by Longevity Power)
- 1 tbsp fresh aloe vera
- dash of salt

directions

1. Prepare the hazelnut mylk, and freeze it in ice cube trays until solid.
2. Blend all of the ingredients in a high-speed blender until it reaches milkshake consistency.
3. Enjoy immediately!

notes

* The nut mylk recipe on page 20 is for a large batch, about 7 cups. You will only need 1 cup of nut mylk to make 6 frozen cubes.

† This ingredient is not raw.

coconut chocolate smoothie

ingredients

smoothie:
- 3 cups raw coconut water
- ½ cup raw coconut meat
- 2 tbsp raw cacao powder
- dash of salt

garnish:
- raw shredded coconut

directions

1. Blend all of the ingredients in a high-speed blender for about 2 minutes, for a silky smooth texture.
2. Garnish with the shredded coconut.
3. Enjoy immediately, or store in the fridge.

notes

You can buy packaged frozen coconut meat and bottled raw coconut water. Or, hack open a fresh young Thai coconut for both water and meat.

vanilla chocolate chunk ice cream

ingredients

vanilla ice cream:
- 10 cubes frozen almond or hazelnut mylk (page 20)*
- 1 tbsp raw lucuma powder
- 1 tbsp raw coconut nectar (or other raw sweetener)
- ½ tsp vanilla powder
- 1 tbsp fresh aloe vera (optional)
- dash of salt

chocolate chunks:
- ¼ cup "ian & jonah's chocolate chips" (page 114)

directions

1. Prepare the almond mylk, and freeze it in ice cube trays until solid.
2. Put the ice cream ingredients in the Vitamix blender.
3. Start the blender on low. Use the tamper to press contents down into blades as you turn it up to high. Continue, until it reaches the consistency of ice cream. Do not over-blend.
4. Add the "ian & jonah's chocolate chips" and blend for a few seconds.
5. Enjoy immediately!

notes

* The nut mylk recipe on page 20 is for a large batch, about 7 cups. You will only need about 1¼ cups of nut mylk to make 10 frozen cubes.

blueberry sage parfait

ingredients

vanilla layer:
- 16 cubes frozen almond mylk (page 20)*
- 3 dates, pitted
- 1 tsp vanilla powder
- 1 tbsp fresh aloe vera (optional)
- 1½ tbsp raw lucuma powder
- dash of salt

blueberry layer:
- ⅓ of vanilla layer
- ⅔ cup fresh blueberries
- 2 tbsp fresh sage leaves

chocolate layer:
- ⅓ vanilla layer
- 2 tbsp raw cacao powder

directions

1. Prepare the almond mylk, and freeze it in ice cube trays until solid.
2. Put the ingredients for the vanilla layer in the Vitamix blender. Start the blender on low. Use the tamper to press contents down into blades as you turn it up to high. Continue, until it reaches the consistency of soft serve.
3. Pour one-third of it into a glass.
4. Set aside another one-third in the freezer.
5. To the remaining one-third in the blender, add the blueberries and sage. Blend for 5 – 10 seconds on high.
6. Pour the blueberry layer into glass, on top of the vanilla layer.
7. Put the vanilla layer from freezer into the blender with the cacao powder and blend for 5 – 10 seconds on high.
8. Pour the chocolate layer into the glass.
9. Enjoy immediately!

notes

* The nut mylk recipe on page 20 is for a large batch, about 7 cups. You only need 2 cups of nut mylk to make 16 frozen cubes.

peppermint cacao shake

ingredients

- 1 cup raw almond or hazelnut mylk (page 20)*
- 6 cubes frozen almond or hazelnut mylk (page 20)*
- 1½ tbsp raw cacao powder
- 1 large date, pitted
- 1 tsp Longevity in a Bottle† (optional)
- 1 tbsp fresh aloe vera gel
- dash of salt
- 2 drops therapeutic-grade organic peppermint essential oil

directions

1. Prepare the almond or hazelnut mylk, and freeze it in ice cube trays until solid.
2. Blend all of the ingredients, except the essential oil, in a high-speed blender, until it reaches milkshake consistency.
3. Add the essential oil and blend for five seconds on low.
4. Enjoy immediately!

notes

* The nut mylk recipe on page 20 is for a large batch, about 7 cups. You will only need 1 cup of nut mylk to make 6 frozen cubes.
† This ingredient is not raw.

Garnish with raw cacao nibs.

basic chocolate shake

ingredients

- 1 cup raw almond or hazelnut mylk (page 20)*
- 6 cubes frozen nut mylk (page 20)*
- 2 tbsp raw cacao powder
- ½ tsp vanilla powder
- 1 date, pitted
- dash of salt

directions

1. Prepare the almond or hazelnut mylk, and freeze it in ice cube trays until solid.
2. Blend all of the ingredients in a high-speed blender, until it reaches milkshake consistency.
3. Enjoy immediately!

notes

* The nut mylk recipe on page 20 is for a large batch, about 7 cups. You will only need 1 cup of nut mylk to make 6 frozen cubes.

Garnish with cacao powder, vanilla powder, and edible flowers for an extra-special presentation.

chocolate dessert balls

THESE RECIPES ARE FUN AND SWEET! KIDS AND FRIENDS WILL ENJOY HELPING YOU HAND-ROLL AND DECORATE THEM. YOU WILL NEED A FOOD PROCESSOR FOR THE RECIPES IN THIS SECTION.

goji pine pollen

ingredients

- 8 large dates, pitted
- ¾ cup fully prepared raw walnuts
- ½ cup raw hemp seeds
- 1 – 2 tbsp raw cacao powder
- ½ tbsp Goji Joy* (by Longevity Power) or raw goji powder
- 1 tsp Maca Bliss* (by Longevity Power) or raw maca powder
- 1 tsp pine pollen
- ¼ tsp turmeric powder
- 1 tsp raw mesquite powder
- 1 tsp raw lucuma powder
- dash of salt

directions

1. Process all of the ingredients together in a food processor, for about 30 seconds. Mixture should be crumbly, and hold together when you squeeze it in your hands.
2. Form the mixture into balls with your hands.
3. Enjoy immediately, or store in the fridge.

notes

For a warm, melt-in-your-mouth treat: try warming in the dehydrator on 115 °F for an hour.

Try rolling them in shredded coconut, goji powder, or pine pollen.

* This ingredient is not raw.

rosemary vanilla

ingredients

- 6 large dates, pitted
- $\frac{1}{2}$ cup raw hemp seeds
- $\frac{1}{2}$ cup raw fully prepared walnuts
- 1 tbsp raw cacao powder
- $1\frac{1}{2}$ tbsp fresh rosemary
- $\frac{1}{2}$ tsp vanilla powder
- $\frac{1}{4}$ tsp salt

directions

1. Process all of the ingredients together in a food processor, for about 30 seconds. Mixture should be crumbly, and hold together when you squeeze it in your hand.
2. Form the mixture into balls with your hands.
3. Enjoy immediately, or store in the fridge.

notes

For a warm, melt-in-your-mouth treat: try warming in the dehydrator on 115 °F for an hour.

This recipe is particularly nice during the fall and wintertime.

Press a single rosemary leaf onto the side for a colorful garnish.

ginger açai

ingredients

dessert balls:
- 6 large dates, pitted
- ½ cup raw hemp seeds
- ½ cup raw fully prepared walnuts
- 1 tbsp raw cacao powder
- 1 tbsp freeze dried açai powder
- ½ inch fresh ginger, peeled
- ¼ tsp salt

garnish:
- grated fresh ginger
- açai powder

directions

1. Process all of the ingredients together in a food processor, for about 30 seconds. Mixture should be crumbly, and hold together when you squeeze it in your hands.
2. Form the mixture into balls with your hands.
3. Garnish with fresh grated ginger.
4. Enjoy immediately, or store in the fridge.

notes

For a warm, melt-in-your-mouth treat: try warming in the dehydrator on 115 °F, without garnish, for an hour. Add the garnish right before serving.

curry

ingredients

dessert balls:
- 6 large dates, pitted
- ½ cup raw hemp seeds
- ½ cup raw fully prepared walnuts or almonds
- 1 tbsp raw cacao powder
- ¼ tsp salt

coating:
- curry powder

directions

1. Process all of the ingredients together in a food processor, for about 30 seconds. Mixture should be crumbly, and hold together when you squeeze it in your hand.
2. Form the mixture into balls with your hands.
3. Put curry powder in small bowl and roll each ball in it until coated.
4. Roll each ball lightly between palms to get off the excess curry powder.
5. Enjoy immediately, or store in the fridge.

notes

For a warm, melt-in-your-mouth treat: try warming in the dehydrator on 115 °F for an hour.

orange

ingredients

dessert balls:
- 6 large dates, pitted
- ½ cup raw hemp seeds
- ½ cup raw fully prepared walnuts
- 2 tbsp raw cacao powder
- 1 tbsp orange zest (must be organic)
- ¼ tsp salt

garnish:
- orange zest (must be organic)

directions

1. Process all of the ingredients together in a food processor, for about 30 seconds. Mixture should be crumbly, and hold together when you squeeze it in your hand.
2. Form the mixture into balls with your hands.
3. Garnish with fresh orange zest.
4. Enjoy immediately, or store in the fridge.

notes

For a warm, melt-in-your-mouth treat: try warming in the dehydrator on 115 °F, without garnish, for an hour. Add the garnish right before serving.

coated blondes

ingredients

blondes:
- 6 large dates, pitted
- ½ cup raw hemp seeds
- ½ cup raw macadamia nuts
- 1 tbsp raw lucuma powder
- ¼ tsp salt

coating:
- ½ batch "basic molded chocolate" recipe (page 26)

toppings:
- fully prepared raw nuts, chopped
- raw shredded coconut
- raw cacao nibs

directions

1. Cover a cutting board or baking sheet with parchment paper.
2. Prepare blondes: process all of the ingredients together in a food processor, for about 30 seconds. Mixture should be crumbly, and hold together when you squeeze it in your hand.
3. Form the mixture into balls with your hands.
4. Put them on parchment paper and chill in the freezer.
5. Prepare half batch of "basic molded chocolate" through Step 2.
6. Remove the blondes from the freezer.
7. With a small bowl or dish underneath to catch the drippings, place a ball on a fork and generously pour chocolate over to coat completely.
8. Put coated ball on the parchment paper and add topping immediately, as the chocolate will begin hardening.
9. Repeat with each ball.
10. Put in the freezer at least 10 minutes to harden chocolate completely.
11. Enjoy immediately, or store in the fridge.

random chocolate fun

SOME RECIPES IN THIS SECTION
REQUIRE A HIGH-SPEED BLENDER,
FOOD PROCESSOR, OR DEHYDRATOR.

chocolate coconut buckwheat granola

ingredients

- 1 ¾ cups raw cashews, soaked 4 − 8 hours (yielding about 2 cups)
- 1 ⅓ cups raw buckwheat groats, soaked 6 hours (yielding about 2 cups)
- 1 tbsp raw coconut oil, melted
- ½ cup pitted dates
- 1 cup raw shredded coconut
- 1 tsp raw mesquite powder
- 2 tbsp raw cacao powder
- 1 tsp vanilla powder
- ½ tsp salt

directions

1. Soak the buckwheat and cashews.
2. Rinse the cashews and buckwheat, and set aside to drain. Make sure to rinse the buckwheat really well, since it creates a slimy gel when soaked.
3. In a food processor, process dates and coconut oil until it becomes a paste.
4. Add remaining ingredients, except cashews & buckwheat, and process until well combined.
5. Transfer the cashews, buckwheat, and paste into a large bowl. Mix together by hand.
6. Spread mixture out loosely onto two dehydrator trays with ParaFlexx sheets.
7. Dehydrate on 115 °F for 24 hours.
8. Enjoy immediately while it's still warm or store in a dry place.

notes

This is a gluten-free recipe.

original cookie, spirulina ball variation, cacao powder ball variation

cacao nib cookies

ingredients

- 2 cups raw shredded coconut (macaroon cut)
- 1 cup fully prepared raw almonds
- ⅓ cup raw buckwheat groats, soaked 6 hours (yielding about ½ cup)
- ½ tsp vanilla powder
- ¼ cup raw coconut nectar
- 2 tbsp raw coconut oil
- 1 tsp salt
- ¼ cup raw cacao nibs

directions

1. In a food processor, process the first four ingredients until the texture is fine, like the shredded coconut.
2. Rinse the buckwheat really well, since it creates a slimy gel when soaked.
3. Add the remaining ingredients and process again, until well combined.
4. Form the mixture into balls by hand. Or, spread out to onto parchment paper ½-inch thick and use cookie cutters.
5. Place the cookies on parchment paper, supported underneath by cutting board or cookie sheet.
6. Put it in the freezer for 30 minutes or one hour in the fridge.
7. Enjoy immediately, or store in the fridge.

notes

Try adding superfood or herbal powders, such as spirulina or raw cacao powder (shown in picture).

Try coating in chocolate (Steps 5 – 12, page 39).

chocolate-dipped fruit & pecans

ingredients

chocolate coating:
- ½ batch "basic molded chocolate" recipe (page 26)

fruit & nuts:
- assorted seasonal fruit
- fully prepared raw pecans

directions

1. Prepare fruit as needed (peel bananas, peel and slice kiwi, etc.).
2. Place the fruit and pecans on a cutting board or plate. Put in the freezer to chill, while you prepare chocolate coating.
3. Prepare "basic molded chocolate" through Step 2.
4. If needed, transfer the chocolate to a small bowl, deep enough to dip into ½-inch.
5. Remove the fruit from the freezer.
6. Cover another cutting board or tray with parchment paper.
7. Dip each piece of fruit ½-inch into the chocolate, allowing the excess to drop off for a few moments.
8. Lay the coated pieces flat on the parchment paper.
9. When all of the pieces are coated, put it in the freezer for 10 minutes to finish hardening the chocolate.
10. Enjoy immediately!

Notes on next page…

notes

Pecans can be stored in cool, dry place. Fruit is best eaten immediately.

Try garnishing with chopped nuts or seeds, shredded coconut, or cacao nibs:

1. Place the freshly dipped fruit onto parchment paper.
2. Sprinkle your garnish onto the section coated with chocolate immediately. You must do this one at a time, right after dipping, or the chocolate will harden and the garnish will not stick.

"Food should be fun."
— Thomas Keller

matt's chocolate shell

ingredients

- ¼ cup raw cacao butter, finely chopped
- ¼ cup raw cacao paste, finely chopped
- 1½ tbsp raw coconut nectar
- dash of salt

directions

1. Melt the cacao butter and cacao paste (use double boiler or dehydrator method).
2. Whisk in the remaining ingredients until smooth.
3. Pour it over a cold dessert, such as ice cream, and watch it harden instantly!

notes

This recipe is dedicated to Matt Larkowski for being such a generous backer on my Kickstarter campaign, which made this book possible! Thanks, Matt!

Recipe is shown on page 70.

chocolate ice cream pie

ingredients

crust:
- 2 cups raw shredded coconut (macaroon cut)
- 2 tbsp extra virgin raw coconut oil
- ¼ cup raw coconut nectar
- ½ cup fully prepared raw almonds
- ½ tsp salt
- 1 tsp raw mesquite powder

filling:
- 1½ batch "basic chocolate ice cream" recipe (page 71)

directions

1. Prepare crust: put all of the crust ingredients in the food processor. Process until nuts have broken up and the texture is fine.
2. Pour the mixture into an 8-inch pie pan. Form the crust with your hands by pressing the mixture evenly into the bottom and up sides of pan.
3. Put crust in freezer to harden.
4. Prepare the filling.
5. Immediately remove crust from freezer and add ice cream filling, spreading evenly, leaving a bit of clean crust at the top.
6. Put in the freezer to set for 30 – 60 minutes.
7. Garnish with seasonal fruit, nuts, "matt's chocolate shell" (page 111), "ian & jonah's chocolate chips" (page 114) or "chocolate caramel sauce" (page 115).
8. Enjoy immediately!

notes

This crust is very sturdy, so make sure to cut all the way through when serving.

Try adding spices, herbs, or superfood powders to the crust or ice cream.

chocolate ice cream pie, ian & jonah's chocolate chips

ian & jonah's chocolate chips

ingredients

- ½ cup raw cacao paste, finely chopped
- 1 tbsp raw coconut nectar
- dash of salt

directions

1. Put parchment paper on a cutting board or tray and put it in the freezer to chill.
2. Melt cacao paste (use double boiler or dehydrator method).
3. Add the remaining ingredients and whisk until mixture becomes thick but not stiff. The consistency should resemble soft frosting.
4. Transfer the chocolate to a small piping bag or squeeze bottle (page 134). If using a squeeze bottle, cut a bit of the tip off for a larger opening, and tap tip down firmly on cutting board or tray to release air bubbles and get chocolate down into the tip.
5. Onto parchment paper, squeeze a small amount of chocolate out. Press down lightly, then lift up to form a chocolate chip. Do this until you have used all of the chocolate.
6. Put it in the freezer for at least 20 minutes to harden.
7. Enjoy immediately, or store in the fridge.

notes

This recipe is dedicated to Sunil Rajan for being such a generous backer on my Kickstarter campaign, which made this book possible! Thanks, Sunil!

Recipe shown on page 113.

chocolate caramel sauce

ingredients

- 8 – 10 dates, pitted
- 1 cup water
- 2 tsp raw cacao powder
- dash of salt

directions

1. Blend all of the ingredients in a high-speed blender until smooth.
2. Use immediately or store in the fridge.

notes

Try this as a topping on any sweet recipe (such as ice cream or dessert wrap). Or, use it to decorate your serving dish, for a thoughtful and artistic presentation.

Recipe shown on page 116.

chocolate dessert wrap, chocolate
caramel sauce

chocolate dessert wraps

ingredients

wraps:
- ¼ cup raw flax seeds
- ½ tsp vanilla powder
- 2 tsp raw cacao powder
- 3 dates, pitted
- ½ cup water
- dash of salt

filling:
- seasonal fruit

directions

1. Grind the flax seeds in a spice grinder or coffee grinder.
2. In a high-speed blender, blend the ground flax with the remaining ingredients, to form a thick batter.
3. Onto dehydrator trays with ParaFlexx sheets, spread ¼ cup of the batter for each wrap, into a thin circle, 5 – 6 inches across.
4. Tap the dehydrator trays on counter to settle batter and release air bubbles.
5. Dehydrate for 7 – 8 hours on 115 °F.
6. Gently peel wraps off of sheet, and put directly on tray, moist side up.
7. Dehydrate for another hour.
8. Fill with seasonal fruit.
9. Fold over like a crepe, fold in thirds like a burrito, or roll up into a cone shape. If you choose the cone option, roll first, then fill with fruit.
10. Enjoy immediately, or store wraps in sealed container or baggy, in a dry place. Use parchment paper between each wrap to prevent sticking.

notes

Try drizzling on "chocolate caramel sauce" (page 115).

chocolate chaga maca mylk

ingredients

chaga tea:
- 4 cups water
- 2 tbsp chaga granules, or one small chunk

mylk:
- 2 cups raw almonds, soaked 12 – 24 hours
- 5 large dates, pitted
- 3 tbsp raw cacao powder
- 4 tsp Maca Bliss* (by Longevity Power) or raw maca powder
- 2 tbsp fresh aloe vera
- 1 tsp vanilla powder
- ½ tsp turmeric powder
- 1 tsp shilajit
- dash of salt

directions

1. Make the chaga tea: warm chaga and water in crock pot (on low) or in a sauce pan, for two hours or more.
2. Remove the tea from heat, and pour through a strainer.
3. Let the tea chill in the fridge.
4. Blend the chaga tea with the almonds and dates for about one minute in a high-speed blender.
5. Strain it through a nut mylk bag, into a large bowl.
6. Blend resulting liquid with the remaining ingredients.
7. Enjoy immediately, or store in the fridge up to 5 days.

notes

*This ingredient is not raw.

savory uses of cacao

SOME RECIPES IN THIS SECTION REQUIRE A BLENDER, FOOD PROCESSOR, OR DEHYDRATOR.

living guacamole with cacao nibs

ingredients

- 1 ripe avocado
- juice from half a lime
- ¼ cup tomato, diced
- 2 tbsp raw sauerkraut
- ¼ tsp salt
- ¼ tsp black pepper
- 1 inch jalapeño, minced, no seeds
- ¼ cup onion, diced
- 1 tbsp fresh cilantro, chopped
- ½ tbsp raw cacao nibs

directions

1. In a small mixing bowl, mash together the avocado and lime juice.
2. Stir in the remaining ingredients.
3. Enjoy immediately, or store in fridge.

creamy kale with cacao nibs

ingredients

kale:
- 1 bundle kale
- 3 – 4 tbsp raw cacao nibs

cream sauce:
- 1 cup raw cashews, soaked 4 – 8 hours
- ½ cup water
- 1 tsp fresh lemon juice
- 1 tsp salt

directions

1. In a high-speed blender, blend the ingredients for the cream sauce, until smooth.
2. Rinse and remove stems from the kale.
3. Chop the kale into medium pieces.
4. In a large bowl, massage the cream sauce into the kale until it becomes soft.
5. Stir in the cacao nibs.
6. Enjoy immediately, or store in the fridge.

notes

To warm: put this prepared recipe in a sealed glass container in the dehydrator for 1 – 3 hours on 115 °F.

To turn this into kale chips, spread one layer thick over dehydrator trays and dehydrate on 115 °F for 24 hours. Store in sealed container, in dry place.

This recipe is meant to be a little bitter and can be eaten as an entrée or as a side dish.

cacao chili, spicy corn chips with cacao nibs

cacao chili

ingredients

"meat":
- ¾ cup raw walnuts, soaked 4 – 8 hours (yields 1 cup)
- ¼ cup raw almonds, soaked 12 – 24 hours (yields ½ cup)
- 1 cup carrot, roughly chopped

veggies:
- ⅔ cup shiitake mushroom, chopped
- ¼ cup red bell pepper, chopped
- ¼ cup green bell pepper, chopped
- 1 cup celery, chopped
- ⅓ cup red onion, chopped
- ½ – 1 cup tomatoes, chopped

sauce:
- 1 tbsp raw goji berries, soaked 30 minutes
- 1 cup sun-dried tomatoes, soaked 30 minutes
- ½ cup soak water (from tomatoes and goji berries)
- 1½ cup tomatoes, chopped
- 1 clove garlic, peeled
- spicy red pepper to taste
- 1 tsp ground cumin
- 1 tbsp lemon juice
- 1 tbsp raw mesquite powder
- ¼ tsp turmeric powder
- 1 tsp salt
- 1 tbsp raw cacao powder
- 1 tbsp extra virgin olive oil (optional)
- 1 tsp raw coconut aminos
- 2 tbsp fresh oregano

continued on next page...

directions

1. Soak the almonds and walnuts.
2. Soak the goji berries and sun-dried tomatoes together for 30 minutes.
3. Prepare the "meat": in a food processor, pulse carrots and almonds about 10 times.
4. Add the walnuts. Process on low for 5 – 10 seconds. Transfer the mixture to a large mixing bowl.
5. Prepare veggies: in a food processor, pulse mushrooms, bell pepper, celery, tomato, and onion 5 times.
6. Add it to "meat" in a large mixing bowl.
7. Prepare the sauce: in a blender, blend sauce ingredients, except oregano, until smooth.
8. Add fresh oregano to blender and blend on low for 5 seconds.
9. Add the sauce to the large mixing bowl, and combine all ingredients well.
10. Enjoy immediately, or store in the in fridge.

"What I've enjoyed most, though, is meeting people who have a real interest in food and sharing ideas with them. Good food is a global thing, and I find that there is always something new and amazing to learn. I love it!"

— Jamie Oliver

spicy corn chips with cacao nibs

ingredients

- 4 cups (20 ounces) organic, raw corn
- 2 medium yellow bell peppers, seeds and stem removed
- 1 tsp turmeric powder
- ½ tsp black pepper
- ½ cup flax seeds
- 1 tbsp salt
- 1½ tbsp raw cacao nibs
- dash of crushed red pepper flakes

directions

1. Grind the flax seeds in spice or coffee grinder.
2. In a food processor, process all of the ingredients, except cacao nibs, until smooth.
3. Stir in the nibs.
4. Spread evenly over 2 dehydrator trays with ParaFlexx sheets, ⅛ inch thick (about 1½ cups batter each tray).
5. Score with a spatula, in shape and size that you desire.
6. Lightly sprinkle on the pepper flakes.
7. Dehydrate on 115 °F for 8 hours.
8. Remove the sheets and flip chips moist side up directly onto trays.
9. Dehydrate on 115 °F for 15 – 16 hours.
10. Enjoy immediately or store in sealed container in dry place.

notes

Try using red, orange, or green bell peppers for extra color in your chips.

Recipe shown on pages 123, 126.

tips & resources

IN THIS SECTION, YOU WILL FIND INFORMATION ABOUT SPECIFIC EQUIPMENT AND TOOLS, HOMEMADE TIPS AND TRICKS, AND MY RECOMMENDATIONS FOR SOURCING INGREDIENTS.

equipment & tools

high-speed blender Vitamix is my preferred high-speed blender. You will need it for ice creams, smoothies, sauces, nut mylks, nut butters, and much more.

knife A good knife is a must. You can use a cleaver for chopping up cacao paste and cacao butter. For everything else, I prefer a medium-sized chef's knife.

food processor For only periodic use at home, it's not necessary to have the highest quality food processor available. If you are looking for the highest quality, I recommend the Robot Coupe.

chocolate molds There are plastic or silicone molds available, in all shapes and sizes. I prefer silicone.

whisk A whisk is very effective when working with melted chocolate. I prefer a 6 – 8 inch whisk.

mixing bowls You will need mixing bowls in a variety of sizes. I most often use a one cup Pyrex.

dehydrator Excalibur brand dehydrators are big, square boxes with removable trays. The trays make it the most useful for the recipes in this book (as well as other raw food cuisine).

offset spatula This tool is great for spreading batters for chips and wraps, easily and evenly, on dehydrator sheets.

strainer or sifter For powders that are clumpy, it helps to sift them before incorporating them into these recipes. You will need a strainer for rinsing nuts and seeds after soaking (the finer, the better).

plastic wrap Plastic wrap is used to line molds for the fudge recipes.

parchment paper Parchment paper is used in several of the recipes. Hardened chocolate doesn't stick to it. That makes for easy cleanup.

ice cream scoop An ice cream scoop isn't necessary, but I love using it for serving the ice creams.

squeeze bottle A squeeze bottle is handy for several of the recipes. It's great for precise decorating, forming chocolate chips, and working with fillings.

make your own mold for chocolate bark

Place some plastic wrap, or parchment paper, on a plate. Or, line any container with edges with plastic wrap. The lining will make for easy cleanup. The wider the container, the thinner the bark. A small container with higher edges will give you more thickness.

piping bag alternatives

sandwich bag

All you need is a plastic sandwich bag and a cup or mug. Open a baggie and put the bottom part into the cup, while you peel the top opening around the rim of the cup.

1. Place prepared mixture into baggie.
2. Pull the bag out of the cup.
3. Squeeze the mixture down into the bottom corner.
4. Twist the top part of the bag, to prevent the mixture from coming out.
5. When ready to use, snip off a small piece of the bottom corner of the baggie, to allow the mixture to come out through the opening.

squeeze bottles

I love using squeeze bottles for decorating my creations. Most have a very narrow tip. You can cut off a bit to create a bigger opening, depending on what you want to use it for.

garnishing

Little extras can be simple, impactful, and easy. Try these tips if you are looking to improve the appearance and appeal of your food and drinks. Food can be fun, gorgeous, yummy, and definitely artistic.

1. Garnish with an ingredient used in the recipe. Some of my favorite simple garnishes include superfood powders (goji, spirulina, cacao), spices (cayenne, turmeric, vanilla, cinnamon), citrus zest, chopped nuts, shredded coconut, fruit, chopped fresh herbs (parsley, cilantro, sage, etc.).
2. Garnish with contrasting colors. Use something bright if the food has a dull color, something dark on light colored food, and something light on dark colored food.
3. Add texture! If a recipe is smooth or flat, adding a garnish with some texture or shape to it can give it some depth. For example: a silky smoothie with cacao nibs, edible flowers, or berries on top.

turn shake recipes into ice cream

My shake recipes are also great as ice creams. Here's how, to convert them, using the Vitamix blender:

1. Substitute nut mylk with 4 – 6 cubes frozen nut mylk (10 – 12 total).
2. Using a tamper to press ingredients down into the blade, blend on high, until it reaches the consistency of ice cream. Stop the blender once or twice to scrape down the sides, and ingredients stuck in the corners. Do not over-blend.

make ice cream with an ice cream maker

My ice cream recipes involve using a Vitamix blender with a tamper. To make them with an ice cream maker instead:

1. In recipe, substitute frozen nut mylk cubes with unfrozen nut mylk. (1 cup milk = 8 cubes, in standard ice cube tray)
2. Blend all ingredients well.
3. Pour into the ice cream maker and let it run, following the directions for that model.

sources for equipment & ingredients

For your convenience, I have created a companion page on my website for this recipe book. It includes:

1. A growing list of physical stores which carry raw cacao, superfood, and herbal ingredients.
2. Direct links to the websites I recommend for ingredients, tools, equipment, and molds.

LaurenAmerson.com/chocolate

My favorite online stores for ingredients:

- Raw Food World
- Earth Circle Organics
- Essential Living Foods
- Raw Vegan Source
- Longevity Power
- Longevity Warehouse
- Live Superfoods
- Ultimate Superfoods

Brands to look for when shopping for ingredients:

- Earth Circle Organics
- Artisana
- Coconut Secret
- Ojio/Ultimate Superfoods
- Divine Organics

glossary

açai A berry with a tart flavor and purple coloring. Commonly sold as a frozen purée or freeze dried powder. Considered a superfood.

bioavailable The ability of a food's nutrients to be assimilated and used by the body.

blue-green algae A particular kind of micro-algae found in Lake Klamath, Oregon. Considered a superfood.

buckwheat A gluten-free grain.

cacao Chocolate in its pure, original, raw, unprocessed form.

camu camu The powdered form of a berry, known for its high Vitamin C content. Considered a superfood.

carob A bean, used in its powdered form, with a similar flavor to chocolate.

chaga A woody tree mushroom, known for its tonic medicinal qualities. It has a slight vanilla flavor and produces a dark tea.

chlorella A green micro-algae, considered a superfood. Known for its high levels of chlorophyl.

cordyceps A medicinal mushroom.

dehydrator A piece of kitchen equipment which can dry (remove moisture from) or melt foods at controlled low temperatures. Very useful in raw vegan cuisine.

essential oils Very potent oils found in plants, used for fragrance and medicinal applications.

goji berry A red berry, typically sold in its dried form, considered a superfood. Has a sweet, tart taste.

lucuma A Peruvian fruit that is low glycemic and has a slight butterscotch flavor. Commonly used in ice cream for its unique flavor and sweetness.

maca A high-elevation, cruciferous root vegetable, grown in the Andes. Known for its benefits to endurance, libido, energy, strength, and the endocrine system.

marbling A technique for creating a swirl design resembling the appearance of marble, in food.

matcha A tea powder with a natural bright green color.

mylk A non-dairy milk alternative, made by blending nuts or seeds with water and straining fiber out with a nut milk bag.

raw food Food that have never been heated above a temperature that is known to destroy vital enzymes, nutrients, and other properties. The general guideline is to never heat above $110 - 118$ °F. There are many books describing the changes that occur when food is cooked.

raw vegan food Food that meets both raw and vegan standards.

shilajit A tar-like mineral compound that adds nutrition and an earthy quality to recipes.

spirulina A kind of micro-algae, considered a superfood.

superfood Foods found to be nutritionally superior.

vegan food Food that doesn't contain any animal products whatsoever. No meat (muscle or organ) from any animal (including fish), no dairy (milk, butter, cream, cheese), no egg, or honey.

zest Scraping small pieces of rind or skin of a citrus fruit, typically.

zeolite clay An edible clay which helps to detoxify heavy metals and other toxins from the body.

index

about the author

Lauren Amerson is a self-taught raw vegan chef. Before raw food beckoned her, she worked as a massage therapist and yoga teacher.

She is also a self-taught artist and loves dancing, horses, organic gardening, tattoos, knitting, nature, and sunshine.

Lauren continues experimenting, and fearlessly playing with her food! Through her videos, classes and online offerings, she enjoys sharing her passion for creativity, health, and transformation!

She looks forward to producing more raw vegan recipe books in the future.

Find her online:

- LaurenAmerson.com
- youtube.com/shaktigoddess1
- etsy.com/shop/shaktigoddess

Madelene Farin did the amazing photographs for this book. You can find more of her beautiful work at her website: MadeleneFarin.com

25329351R00088

Printed in Poland
by Amazon Fulfillment
Poland Sp. z o.o., Wrocław